QWOTES

"Don't be upset that they caught your mistake. Be happy that you caught their attention."

Daniel M. Lewis

Copyright © 2019 Daniel Lewis

All rights reserved.

ISBN: 9781696781312

DEDICATION

This book is dedicated to my lovely wife Renata and my two little boys, Jacob and Benjamin. Every quote in this book represents a time, a feeling and an emotion that I've experienced in my pursuit of creating the best life possible for you. My goal is to make you happy, proud and to always keep a smile in your hearts.

One day I hope you will look back and say,

"Daddy did his best to live an exemplary life; one that demonstrates the love of God, hard work and the genuine care for the well-being of others, just like Jesus did."

You're my reason for waking up early and my reason for going days without sleep. Your happiness gives me joy beyond measure and I can confidently say that I am the most successful man on earth because you are my legacy.

I love you.

Table Of Contents

How To Use This Book 1
Acknowledgments 2
The Realities of Entrepreneurship 35
Sacrifice 72
About The Author 140

QWOTES

How To Use This Book

This book was designed to offer inspiration and motivation to the reader. However, my intention with this book is to also allow you, the reader to take each quote and personalize it for yourself. Make these quotes real to you and your situation.

How to accomplish this?

Every page includes a quote and then offers the reader ample space to sketch, draw, cut and paste or insert their own image, icon or symbol based on their interpretation of the quote. Once you've illustrated an image to match the quote, share the image on your social media channels using the hashtag **#DLQWOTES**. Get creative, become the illustrator, express your creativity and have fun making this book uniquely yours!

After all,

"Quotes are just words, until you make them come alive."

- D. Lewis

Acknowledgments

It is impossible for me not to thank my dad and mom for being my primary source of inspiration and motivation. This book is a result of the words of wisdom that you have spoken to me over the years. Every time I was down, you had a ready word to pick me up. When I was confused, you simplified business and life for me. All of these things have made me into the man I am today. If I was to write about all the ways you have impacted my life from a child until now, I could easily fill a library. With that being said, the most important gift you given me thus far is the knowledge of Jesus Christ, my Lord and my Saviour. He is the real hero and the main source of everything I know and every inspiring word that I've shared in this book. Thank you for introducing me to Him. He is the best gift you could ever offer to me.

To my brother Jonathan and his lovely wife Natalie and all their beautiful daughters (Shanice, Abigail and Ruth-Anne.) You have made me the world's happiest uncle. To my sister Rachel, you tease me like crazy as your way of showing how much you love me. The feeling is mutual… Sort of. To my close friends and those who have shared in my success and trials for many years, thank you a million times over.

QWOTES

Greatness is always one step further.

- D. Lewis

QWOTES

People judge you quickly, so you might as well live in the fast lane.

- D. Lewis

QWOTES

When nobody cared,

I would sing it to the chairs.

- D. Lewis

QWOTES

When skyscrapers become LEGO pieces, you're dreaming big!

- D. Lewis

QWOTES

I use to get sent to the office.

Now I get invited.

- D. Lewis

Want to be successful?

Get ready to miss a few parties.

- D. Lewis

Haters:

First they'll laugh at you,

and then they'll quote you.

- D. Lewis

QWOTES

You're as BIG as the impact you leave behind.

- D. Lewis

Our greatest success is our ability to impact others in a positive way.

- D. Lewis

QWOTES

When her "perfect date" requires laptops and blueprints, #ShesTheOne.

- D. Lewis

Oh I'm sorry... I forgot how to be lazy.

- D. Lewis

It's 3:40 A.M. if you're reading this, you're either very successful or very stressed out.

- D. Lewis

Drink tea and build things.

- D. Lewis

Never speak your mind,

only speak your heart.

- D. Lewis

If your success is money,

then your success is limited.

- D. Lewis

Strive for consistency, not perfection.

- D. Lewis

Life gives you the instruments,

you create the song.

- D. Lewis

Trendy is cool. Timeless is forever.

- D. Lewis

Bedtime is when the birds start chirping.

- D. Lewis

Humility is often discovered

when you are on a plane.

- D. Lewis

Want to help someone? Don't tell them what you know, instead share with them what you've learned.

- D. Lewis

QWOTES

Whatever it takes, I'll get there.

- D. Lewis

Life is a book with blank pages, as we live out our life, the story is created.

- D. Lewis

QWOTES

First you're weird,

and then you're the standard.

- D. Lewis

The **NEXT** generation is the **NOW** priority.

- D. Lewis

Life is an empty canvas and you're not born as an artist. Learn the skills needed to create a beautiful life.

- D. Lewis

Life is not beautiful,
unless you make it beautiful.

- D. Lewis

When the message is real,

the impact is obvious.

- D. Lewis

You grind hard,

let the night be your witness.

- D. Lewis

When they're working, you're working.
When they're sleeping, you're working.
This is the difference.

- D. Lewis

I write books on planes, while others watch movies and sleep. I'm not better than they are, perhaps I'm just more hungry.

- D. Lewis

The Realities of Entrepreneurship

Entrepreneurship is…

95% hard work and 5% perks.

Every day you are one day away from failing and everyday you are one day away from success.

It's all determined on your efforts.

Your efforts are driven by your passion.

Your passion is fueled by your purpose. If you have no purpose, you're not an entrepreneur… On the contrary, you're a person trying to escape their 9-5 reality, thinking that running your own business is the easy way out.

It usually takes about 24 months to realize that you were wrong.

Oh yes, so let's talk about those perks shall we?

Along the entrepreneurial journey you will stay at the finest hotels, but that's only because it's a closer commute to the Conference Centre where you'll be required to **work** the next morning.

You will fly business class, but that's only because you'll need the extra privacy and quiet to prepare for your next presentation. (a.k.a work)

You will drive a nice car... but that's only because you don't have time to be in and out of mechanic shops everyday while your business needs you.

You will meet celebrities... but that's only based on the extremely slim chance that you have something they might actually need or appreciate, and you can convince them that your product is a must have, within the very strict 40 seconds you're given to speak to them.

You will dress in quality clothes, but that's only because you won't be admitted into many of the venues you'll need to attend for that important networking meeting in average casual apparel.

With all these "perks" on the table, there is still an 88% chance that within the first 5 years your business will close down.

If these odds are still appealing to you... then you should probably start writing your business plan and get ready to grind.

- D. Lewis

In business you're one day away from failure and one day away from success.
Still interested?

- D. Lewis

Don't prove them wrong.

Prove yourself right.

- D. Lewis

Time is a precious thing... don't waste it on satisfying other people's preconceived opinions about you. Prove yourself to yourself, that's all the proof you need.

- D. Lewis

What did you do today?
The future is watching.

- D. Lewis

I'm not **JUST** an entrepreneur,

I'm a storyteller.

- D. Lewis

I'm not successful because I have a store. I'm successful because I still mop my store.

- D. Lewis

Sometimes the best reflection

is that without mirrors.

- D. Lewis

Be crazy. It looks good on you.

- D. Lewis

QWOTES

If you're not winning, you're waiting, if you're waiting... what are you waiting for?

- D. Lewis

There is one check that can change your entire life... a reality check.

- D. Lewis

Do it, if it's real to you.

- D. Lewis

Never be afraid to do it alone

- D. Lewis

You begin to succeed the moment you realize it takes more than hard work to make it. Be allergic to failure.

- D. Lewis

Hard work alone is not the differentiating trait between successful people and those who are looking for success. People who are successful see failure as a sickness. It would be better to die trying, than to live, wishing that you tried.

- D. Lewis

Sometimes we have to trade in the good family days for the good family life.

- D. Lewis

Tall mountains can be small hills,

depending on your perspective.

- D. Lewis

QWOTES

Your effort is the best indicator of your interest.

- D. Lewis

Effort speaks louder than words.

- D. Lewis

A true smile begins in the heart and can be seen in the eyes.

- D. Lewis

When you start a business you don't become an entrepreneur, you become

a problem solver.

- D. Lewis

QWOTES

Although expectation is a good thing, mystery is equally impactful.

- D. Lewis

Never get trapped in the trend you started, because you then forfeit the freedom of creativity. Do it, and when you don't feel like doing it anymore, don't. This will keep you in the pilots seat.

- D. Lewis

If you lose the mystery, you lose the magic.

- D. Lewis

Behind every dream there's a person.

Behind every success there's a people.

- D. Lewis

Oh how I've hustled.

- D. Lewis

Start at home base.

Work one area at a time.

Then connect the dots.

- D. Lewis

STAR POWER!
It's your secret weapon in business and in life. Use it.

- D. Lewis

Never let your corporate status cloud your human conscience.

- D. Lewis

I aim to stay true to the grade 3 me. The me that cared when someone was having a bad day in class or feeling left out of a group activity. Money and status should never change these things.

- D. Lewis

QWOTES

Or you can not do it and live with regrets.

- D. Lewis

Find beauty in what you do.

- D. Lewis

Winning is not a feeling of comfort, but rather a reward of extreme effort given.

- D. Lewis

QWOTES

Successful people perform and then perfect.

- D. Lewis

They go to the club.
You learn how to open one.
#TheDifference.

- D. Lewis

Sacrifice

Email after Email, chapter after chapter, client after client, customer after customer, presentation after presentation... it takes SACRIFICE. Every night I watch the hands on the clock race to the next number until the moon disappears and the sun takes center stage. I try to sleep for a couple hours but I'm usually woken up by the sound of ringtones and ping notifications. I wipe the tiredness out of my eyes, fix myself up, hit the kettle and steep a delicious tea. As I sit at my desk and think about the privilege of life, my family and the people I can potentially impact as I travel through this life. Then I consider the sacrifice, and say to myself "let's do it all over again."

- *From the book HOW? By Daniel M. Lewis*

Your <u>style</u> is:
Single and looking.

Find it.
Marry it.
Own it.

- D. Lewis

When you diversify your image, you transform your game.

- D. Lewis

Live with the consciousness of every decision you make, so you never look back with regret."

- D. Lewis

Never thinking luxury.

Always thinking legacy.

- D. Lewis

A successful person is not defined by what they acquired here, but rather what they left behind.

- D. Lewis

Neglecting reflection is lethal in business.

- D. Lewis

In the pursuit of success, it is important to stop, reflect, correct and proceed. This is the way of champions.

- D. Lewis

See it.

- D. Lewis

My secret to success is no secret.

I just focus on giving.

- D. Lewis

The world we live in is simply a result of the choices you and I make everyday.

- D. Lewis

Successful ventures start with a dream and transition into a mission.

- D. Lewis

Everything in your business should be fashionable and infused with your personal style.

- D. Lewis

Want to build an empire?
Focus on building someone first.

- D. Lewis

Smiling even through the toughest of times displays ones true strength.

- D. Lewis

QWOTES

When your attachment to money is so close that you are valued and defined by your money, then everything that can happen to your money can happen to you:

Devalued. Used.

Taken for granted...

Learn to make the distinction between YOU having money and money having YOU!

-D. Lewis

QWOTES

When it comes to my competitors, it doesn't matter if I think my products are better or that I have better service.. all that matters is the fact that I want it more than they do. Your work ethic is your only weapon.
#PerfectYourGame

- D. Lewis

On Jan 1st you promised to take over the world and make this your year...

how's that going?

- D. Lewis

QWOTES

Thanks Dad.

- D. Lewis

Thanks Mom.

- D. Lewis

Life is the greatest teacher,

because you can't skip its classes.

- D. Lewis

That's life. Get back up.

- D. Lewis

QWOTES

Mission statement: Make magic.

- D. Lewis

I'm not the smartest in the room.
I don't know my IQ score.
I don't have any diplomas on my wall.
I'm not the best dressed at the party.
I'm not the wealthiest man at the conference.

I'm not always sure about what to do with my business. But if there's one thing I am for sure... I'm a hustler.

Just give me some time.

- D. Lewis

We only go around this thing once.

- D. Lewis

The Slingshot Theory: Our setbacks in life are designed to propel us farther ahead.

- Dad Lewis

People often ask me, "Daniel what's your 5-10 year plan?"

My response..."I'll cross that bridge when I get there."

Living in the present: is the best plan for the future. In 2009 I overcame a nearly tragic situation where my entire life, thoughts, plans, goals and perspectives were drastically brought to a halt. What started out as a casual 2-minute walk to the store across the street, turned into a fight for my life and the fight of my life.

Lesson learned: Instead of categorizing individuals who don't have the "perfect answer" for the questions of the future into a group of unpreparedness, we should first understand that maybe, just maybe... their goal is to enjoy every single day, hour, minute and moment that they have been so graciously granted to the best of their ability.

Now is all we have.

Business school won't teach you that. Experience will.

- D. Lewis

Find your style and use it.

- D. Lewis

To be successful you must first understand that there is no substitute for the grind.

- D. Lewis

When people talk negative about you, just drop it into 3rd gear. #SeeYaLater

- D. Lewis

Talent doesn't get you anywhere, consistency does.

- D. Lewis

When we change our perspective about BIG things, then we understand that BIG is a very small word. It's the little things that count.

- D. Lewis

Don't change the rules.

Make the rules.

- D. Lewis

I only go to parties

if I'm nominated for an award.

- D. Lewis

Don't pay attention to negative people, eventually they'll have to pay to get your attention.

-D. Lewis

Show me how successful you are... but don't show me how BIG your wallet is, show me how BIG your impact is. Our greatest success is our ability to impact others in a positive way.

- D. Lewis

Work when you must, until you can work when you choose.

- D. Lewis

I learned that in life if you're not building something, your probably breaking something down. Build something, even if that something is you.

- D. Lewis

QWOTES

I try never to speak from my mind because it's usually guided by feelings and emotions, which change regularly. Instead, I endeavor to always speak from my heart, because it's guided by truth.

Truth cannot change.

-D. Lewis

You can't print my success.
You can't break it and make change.
You can't devalue my success depending on how well the stock market is doing.

Success is not defined by money. Success is that moment when you can share something you love with someone you love.

-D. Lewis

QWOTES

If you strive for perfection and find it, great, but if you can't maintain it,

you've gained nothing.

Strive for consistency.

Create habits. Create patterns.

- D. Lewis

Instruments don't make songs. People do. Stop complaining and start using the tools around you to create your success.

- D. Lewis

I've dialogued with many aspiring "entrepreneurs" throughout my business journey and I can usually tell when I'm talking to a winner or a loser. The losers blame people and blame circumstances. The winners on the other hand are too busy using life's lemons to make lemonade.

- D. Lewis

Everything I do, I think it's so important, It's the biggest deal, there's nothing like it on earth. Then I go on a plane, and all my "high thoughts" become abased. Having a hard time with being prideful? Book a flight and gain some perspective.

- D. Lewis

I'm not afraid to ask for help when I can't seem to figure it out. I'm not independent. No one is. We all depend on someone or something.

- D. Lewis

QWOTES

I once heard someone say to another person, "I don't need you to give me a ride, I'll take the bus, because I'm independent!" What that person failed to realize is that they still have to depend on the bus driver.

- D. Lewis

Magical is the new ordinary.

Do something special.

- D. Lewis

Show people something real.

- D. Lewis

You want to be successful? You want to grow an empire? You want everyone in the world to buy your products? Here's your homework: Sell one first.

- D. Lewis

Impact. Stay dedicated to it.

- D. Lewis

My business plan was simple. I'm going to let all my business decisions be guided by love. Update: it's working.

- D. Lewis

It's real to me even when I can't touch it.

- D. Lewis

Got an idea? So does everybody else in the world. Do something about it!

- D. Lewis

QWOTES

Great ideas are the same as no ideas, until you act on them.

- D. Lewis

Eat Thai food. Drink tea & inspire others.

- D. Lewis

No one looks back on their life and remembers the amount of nights they got plenty of sleep.

- D. Lewis

If nothing about living excites you,

you are hopeless.

- D. Lewis

If your dreams aren't coming true,

dream different.

- D. Lewis

Life is like surfing, ride the wave.

  - D. Lewis

Be forever gnarly dude!

- D. Lewis

Is it a good idea or a bad one? You'll never know until you explore it.

- D. Lewis

Are you really grinding? Be honest.

- D. Lewis

QWOTES

When's the last time you sweat for it?

- D. Lewis

You'll never get there, unless you see yourself there first.

- D. Lewis

QWOTES

Against all odds. This is the motto I live by.

- D. Lewis

You are not successful because you did what was right. You are successful because you did what you believe.

- D. Lewis

QWOTES

Stay focused on your end goal and your everyday mission.

- D. Lewis

If they say it can be done, it can be done.

- D. Lewis

About The Author

Daniel spent a large portion of his childhood and teenage years chasing a career in music. After making a local name for himself in the rap and hip-hop community, Daniel went on to perform at many music venues throughout Canada and in the U.S. During his pursuit of building a name and image in music, it seemed that Daniel had unfortunately made some negative relationships based on some of the content in his music. In 2009, Daniel became the victim of a nearly fatal stabbing, being stabbed four times on account of one of the messages in one of his songs four years prior to the event. Luckily, Daniel survived the aggravated assault, and would eventually go on to use this tragic situation as momentum to inspire change, first for himself and then for others.

About a year and a half after the stabbing incident, Daniel went on to start a tea company called T By Daniel. The idea was inspired by his new found passion of finding or creating a tool to impact people's lives in a positive way, as his life had been so positively impacted by the many people who aided him during his unfortunate circumstance and also his new love and appreciation of the health benefits that tea had to offer. It seemed crazy at first, but Daniel decided to launch a tea company built on the foundation of impacting people's lives in an unforgettable way.

More than eight years later, the mission continues to prove itself! T By Daniel went on to win a numerous amount of awards recognizing business and community excellence, Daniel and his wife and business partner Renata, have even gone on to serve their teas to many celebrities, dignitaries, entertainers, superstars and even HRH (His Royal Highness) The Prince Of Wales - Prince Charles, and Camilla - The Duchess of Cornwall during their Royal Tour for Canada's 150th celebration.

The goal remains the same to this day, to inspire and impact people's lives in a positive way, using tea as the means to do it, one cup at a time.

Daniel refers to his personal story as one of tragedy to triumph.

Other Books by The Author

How? By Daniel M. Lewis (Autobiography)
He went from tragedy to triumph, now he tells How!
Available on Amazon.ca | Chapters Indigo Brampton

Weird As Waldo

Marketing 101 | How to stand out in the noise

Available on Amazon.ca

For more info contact DanielSpeaks.ca

www.ingramcontent.com/pod-product-compliance
Lightning Source LLC
Chambersburg PA
CBHW060844220526
45466CB00003B/1229